Quick Guide to Hedge Funds

What they are, how they work and why they work

Gina Heng & Seunghyun Cho

ISBN-10: 9810730276
ISBN-13: 978-9810730277

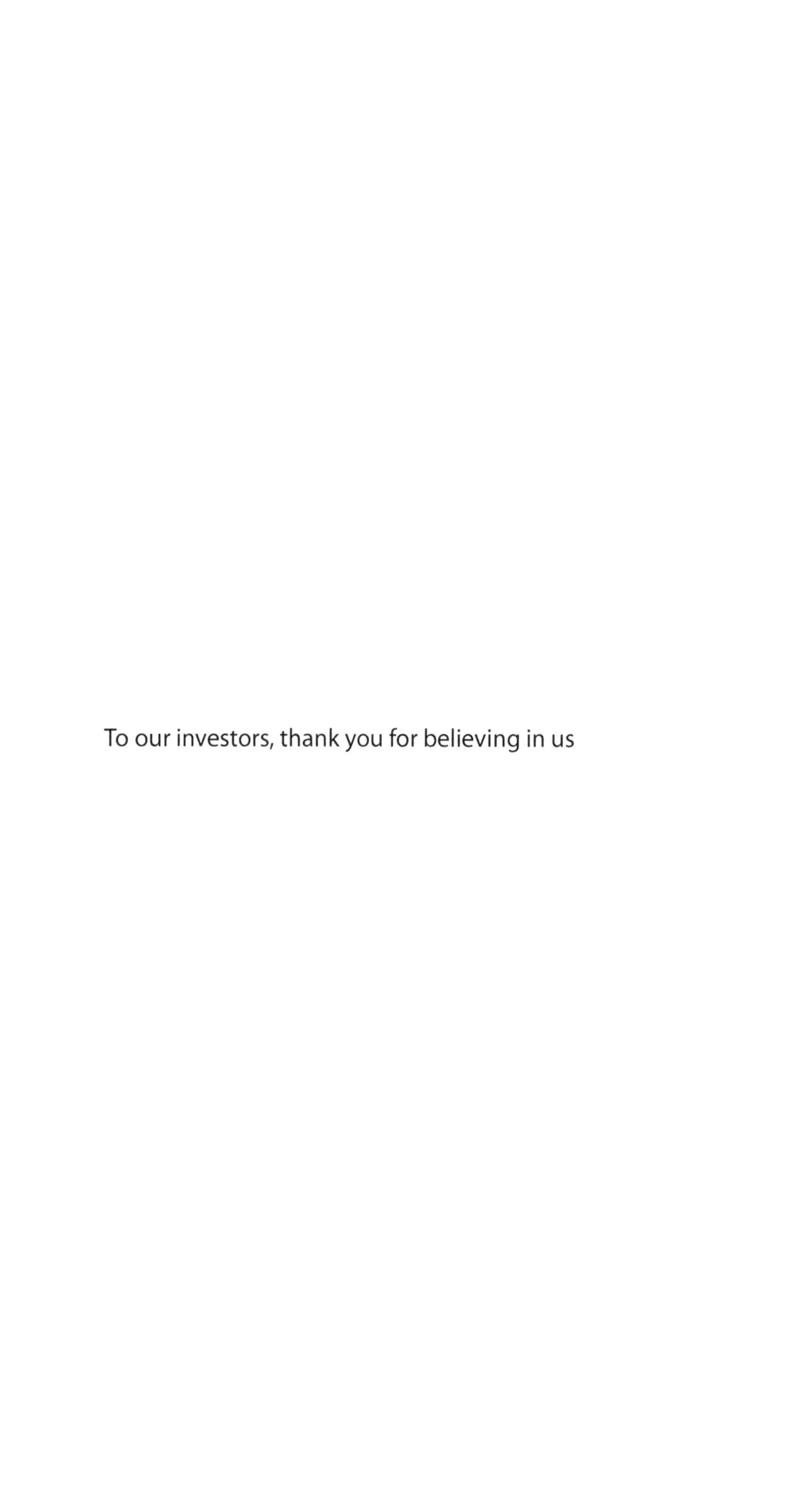

To our investors, thank you for believing in us

CONTENTS

ACKNOWLEDGMENTS

We would like to thank all our families, friends, and business associates for all the support they have been giving us along the way. Special thanks to Bob Lau and Arun Kant who have been a great force in our team. In addition, we would like to thank the LHC Korea team, namely Jaemok Lee, Moonhyun Cho and Deagun Yoon. And much thanks to our very dedicated research associates, Shane Shin, Peter Lee, Minhyoung Kim, and Angela Jong. Finally, we would like to thank Joel Ko of One Asia Investment Partners.

Gina Heng & Seunghyun Cho
Seoul
September 2012

DISCLAIMER

The information provided in this book is informational only and is not an offer to sell or to solicit to any person or entity. These materials are not intended to constitute legal, tax, or accounting advice or investment recommendations. Prospective investors should consult their own advisors regarding such matters. The information herein is subject to change without notice and is not complete with respect to any of the hedge funds described or data supplied; including important disclosures and risk factors associated with an investment in hedge funds, and asset under management sizes. In the case that the information reported is outdated or incorrect, we have no obligation to update or correct such outdated or incorrect information.

There can be no assurance that an investment in hedge funds will achieve profits or avoid incurring losses. This book does not take into account the financial circumstances or the goals of individual investors. Before making an investment decision, an investor and/or its adviser should (i) consider the suitability of alternative investments with respect to its investment objectives and personal situation and (ii) consider factors such as its personal net worth, income, age, risk tolerance, and liquidity needs. Short-term investors and investors who cannot bear the loss of some or all of their investment or the risks associated with the limited liquidity of an investment should not invest.

CHAPTER ONE

Introduction

Given that for a long time, hedge funds have been viewed as secretive, high-risk investments that are exclusive to ultra-high-net worth individuals only; this book has been designed to provide an easy and straightforward understanding of hedge funds. We seek to educate both professionals who wish to get a first look into this segment of the industry as well as novice investors who want to understand more about hedge fund investing.

Despite the industry's mysterious image, a growing number of individuals and institutions have come to perceive hedge funds as a way to improve the overall performance and returns of their investment portfolios, and/or reduce the risk over the years. Even the more conservative pension funds and endowment funds, such as Harvard University's, the world's richest school, have been allocating part of their portfolios to hedge funds in recent times[i].

Since A. W. Jones founded the very first hedge fund, whose focus was to "hedge" with respect to overall market movements in 1949, hedge funds have since been developed to include a variety of functions that are unique to private equity, venture capital, and mutual funds, but operate under fewer regulations. It is difficult to generalize about hedge funds, but they generally pursue various strategies and employ a wide range of assets.

At the end of 2011, assets under management of the global hedge funds industry totaled $1.9 trillion from $118.2 billion ten years earlier.[ii] We expect the industry to only grow larger as global investors become more sophisticated and regulators learn to use hedge funds to deepen their markets in the long run.

CHAPTER TWO

Hedge Funds — the Basics

Investment style

Hedge funds are collective pools of money, or simply a significant sum of money that comes from a sole individual or organization, that are managed by a third-party individual or institution. In general, the main aim is to gain absolute returns on the funds rather than relative returns. This means an actual increase in investment amount rather than merely outperforming a market benchmark that is in the negative. Hedge funds do so by reducing volatility and risk while attempting to preserve capital and deliver positive returns under all market conditions. To achieve these objectives, hedge funds use various investing strategies and different investment products; hedge funds can manage public and private securities and derivative instruments on those securities. They can also take both long and short positions, and may apply leverage (see chapter four for details on the different strategies).

Investment culture

Hedge fund firms tend to be small organizations owned and managed by only one or two key individuals. This exhibits a "smaller is better" culture. There are many similar funds in Asia as well. However, their clientele tends to be focused on high-net-worth individuals as opposed to large institutional investors, especially since the industry is still in its early developmental stages. In a sense, the relationship between the hedge fund manager and client can be closer given that a direct communication channel can be formed. That being said, there are also large hedge funds with a sizable number of staff. We see more of those in the United States and Europe, where the hedge fund industries are more developed.

Investment structure

Hedge funds use different fund structures and systems to make their strategies available to investors. The hedge fund could be in the form of an offshore fund, a limited partnership, a commodity pool, a separate, or a managed account.

The general/limited partnership model is the most common structure for the pool of investment funds that makes up a hedge fund. In this structure, the general partner (fund manager) takes responsibility for the operations of the fund, while limited partners make investments into the partnership and are liable for only paid-in amounts. As a rule, a general/limited partnership must have at least one general partner (GP) and one limited partner (LP), but it can have multiple GPs and many LPs. In this sense, the typical hedge fund structure consists of two tiers.

Figure 1: Typical Hedge Fund Structure

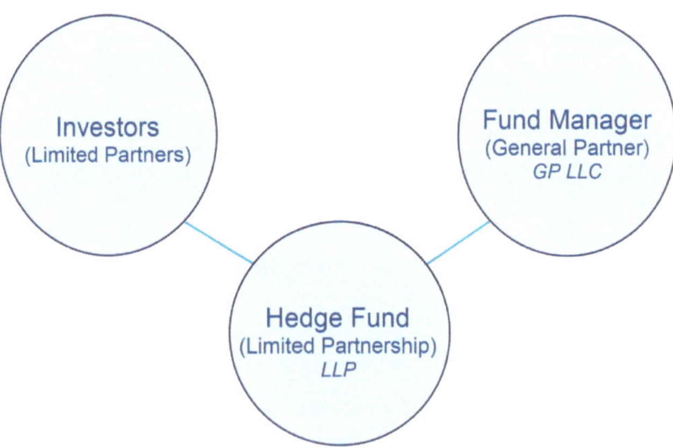

Open-ended nature

Hedge funds are mostly open-ended. This means that the fund will accept further investments and allow investors to withdraw their money from the fund. On the other hand, in close-ended funds, money is raised from the start and is only used to invest.

For an open-ended fund structured as a company, shares will be both issued and redeemed at the net asset value (NAV) per share. If the value of the underlying investments has increased (that means NAV per share has also increased), then the investor will receive a larger sum on redemption than the initial investment. As for a fund structured as a limited partnership, the investor's account will be allocated its portion of any increases or decreases in the NAV of the fund, which will be reflected in the amount of capital that the investor can withdraw.

Fund domicile

The domicile of a hedge fund does not have to be the same as that of its fund manager, administrator, or custodian. Factors such as reducing costs and creating the appropriate fund structure for the investor are more important in deciding where to domicile a fund. In addition, some institutional investors may be bound by rules that limit investment to regulated jurisdictions, while others do not face such requirements. Figure 2 below shows an example of a hedge fund and its domicile in relation to the other parties involved.

Hedge funds are generally domiciled in a couple of locations worldwide. In the United States, hedge funds tend to be located in Delaware. There are also several popular locations in the Caribbean and Europe, including the British Virgin Islands, the Cayman Islands, Guernsey, Bermuda, the Isle of Man, Jersey, Luxembourg, and Dublin. In Asia, fund managers are more likely to domicile their funds in Hong Kong, Australia, Japan, and Singapore. More recently, fund managers have been moving their funds to jurisdictions such as Malta. Single-strategy managers tend to domicile their fund in traditional Caribbean locations and Bermuda, due to lower costs and lighter regulatory.

It is estimated that around half of all hedge funds in 2011 were registered offshore. Cayman Islands was the leading location, accounting for 33 percent of the number of global hedge funds. It was followed by the United States with 23 percent, Luxembourg with 13 percent, Ireland with 7 percent, British Virgin Islands with 5 percent, and Bermuda with 3 percent[iii].

Figure 3: Distribution of Hedge Fund Domiciles by Number of Funds January 2012

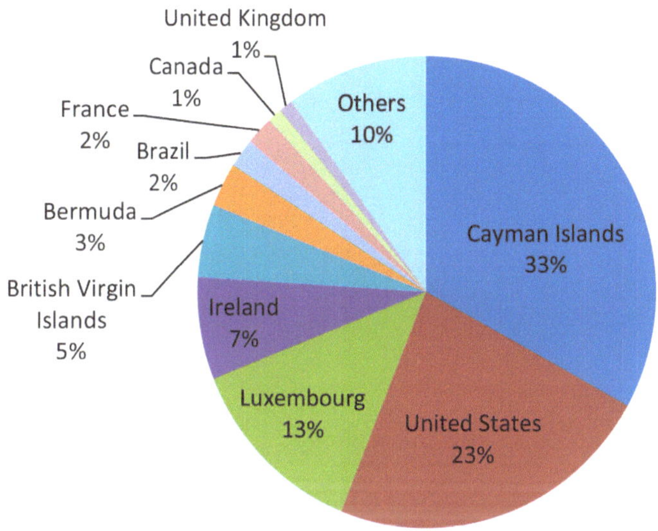

Source: Eurekahedge

Location of fund managers

The United States is the largest center for hedge funds, managing around 70 percent of global assets at the end of 2011. Europe followed with 21 percent and Asia accounted for most of the remainder[iv].

Figure 4: Location of Hedge Fund Managers by Number of Funds, January 2012

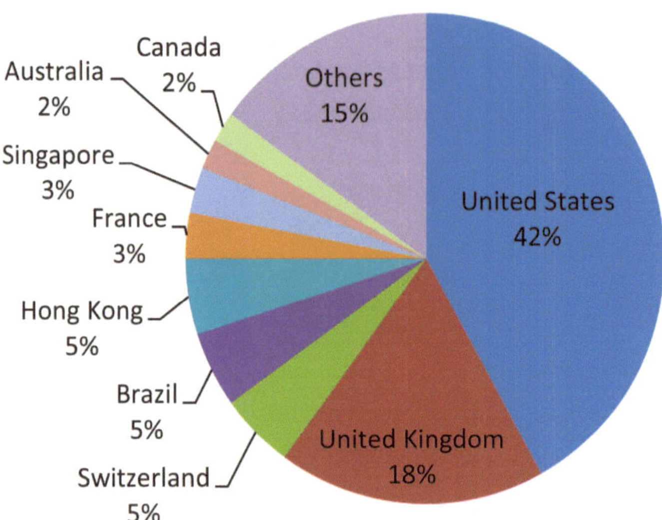

Source: Eurekahedge

CHAPTER THREE

Differences between Hedge Funds and Mutual Funds

The similarities between hedge funds and mutual funds are limited to a few points. First, they are both pooled vehicles for investing in equities, bonds, options, and a variety of other securities. Secondly, they both utilize fund managers to manage a portfolio in which the manager chooses securities and investment strategies that he or she believes will perform the best. The funds are then sold to investors who gain immediate access to a diversified and professional managed portfolio.

Aside from these similarities, hedge funds and mutual funds are very different. The range of investment strategies that hedge funds use, as well as the types of positions they can take, are quite broad and can be very complex relative to mutual funds.

For instance, within the mutual fund world, it is a matter of difference between a money market fund and a balanced fund that invests in both equities and bonds with a pure equity fund that focuses on a broad or specific range of stocks (i.e., small cap Chinese equities).

Within the hedge fund world, other than sector or geographical considerations, hedge fund managers deploy various trading tactics to outwit the markets. For example, there could be differences between a market-neutral equity fund that specializes in Asia and a trend-following global asset allocator fund that takes on highly leveraged positions. Table 1 illustrates the differences between hedge funds and mutual funds.

In short, compared to mutual funds, hedge funds:

- Are private investment vehicles for sophisticated/qualified investors
- Have more concentrated portfolios with fewer holdings
- Use derivatives more frequently
- May take long or short positions in securities
- Use leverage, sometimes in excessive amounts
- Invest in non-public securities

Table 1: Summary of hedge funds and mutual funds

	Hedge Funds	Mutual Funds
Objective	Absolute return	Relative return
Strategies	Minimal limitation, free to include leverage, short selling, and other hedging strategies	Limitations on leverage, short selling, etc.
Primary sources of return and risk	Strategy and manager (alpha)	Market (beta)
Volatility	Historically less than equities	Similar to benchmark index
Culture	Lean and flexible	Large and cumbersome
Liquidity	Limitations on investment and redemption (some managers are moving toward a more liquid approach in light of a more depressed market condition)	Daily liquidity
Marketing	Limitations on marketing and selling	Broad access to the retail market
Business relationship	Client is viewed as a business partner	Manager is agent for client
Fees	Asset-based and performance-based	Asset-based only
Valuation	Usually monthly or quarterly	Daily
Investment Amount	Varies-depends on structure	As low as $1000
Information Transparency	Relatively lower	Relatively higher
Taxation	Pass-through entity, no or minimal tax at fund level	No tax at fund level if all income distributed.

Investment objectives

For any investor, the basic goal of any investment is to deliver a return that will exceed the inflation rate over the investment period, so that the real purchasing power of the investment will increase over time.

As the mutual fund management industry is highly competitive, fund companies aim to attract business (new inflow of money to their funds) by showing how their funds beat a designated target rate of return. For example, an equity mutual fund seeks to beat two targets. First, it seeks to surpass the rate of return achieved by competitors, and secondly, the return of a relevant market index. So, what the mutual fund manager seeks to do is to perform better than other managers in his or her investment style category. For instance, a U.S. cap value fund would want to beat other large cap value funds, but would not mind if it lagged behind some cap growth funds.

Also, the mutual fund manager seeks to beat a passive market benchmark, such as the S&P 500. The benchmark shows the performance of the basic market that the fund is investing in. For example, if the manager delivers 8 percent while the benchmark earns 6 percent, the manager will be pleased with his performance. However if the manager loses 5 percent while the benchmark loses 8 percent, the manager would still be pleased with his performance, even though the investor has lost money. This is because what the mutual fund manager seeks to do is to deliver a good performance relative to the passive benchmark, which may have experienced negative returns.

Hedge funds are different from mutual funds primarily because of the reason mentioned above. Although there are various strategies with different focuses, hedge funds tend to focus on absolute returns only. What they seek is to earn a positive return, not to beat a benchmark. Very simply, a more risk-adverse hedge fund manager may target 10–12 percent annually (net of fees), while a more aggressive manager may try to earn 25–30 percent (net of fees). Overall, both are still seeking positive returns. As a result, many hedge fund managers develop strategies that are not dependent on the market (e.g., constructing a portfolio with a low correlation to an equity market index). Hedge fund managers do not need to depend on what standard markets are doing in order to deliver positive results; this is a trait known as market neutrality. However, not all hedge funds can deliver good news year after year; some fail. And in these cases, they cannot use the excuse that they have beaten some market benchmark after a negative performance.

Investment strategies

Take a U.S. equity-focused mutual fund as an example. The fundamental strategy of the manager is to buy stocks that he or she believes would outperform the fund's designated benchmark—say the S&P 500 index. However, mutual funds operate under specific rules defined by each market jurisdiction. For instance, U.S. mutual funds are subject to rules under the Securities and Exchange Commission (SEC). These rules may be deemed by the market regulators as necessary to protect investors, but they also limit the manager's freedom. The important limitations relate to liquidity, short selling, and diversification. Hedge funds are generally not subject to such limitations. In fact, they do make use of derivatives, leverage, and short selling to reduce risk as well as to generate higher returns (see chapter four on hedge fund styles and themes).

Fee structures

Another primary difference between hedge funds and mutual funds is the fee structure. Hedge funds typically employ a 2/20 rule—2 percent on management fee and the other 20 percent on performance fee (explained in detail in chapter eight), whereas mutual funds charge only the management fee (rates vary). This means that hedge funds are more incentivized to perform well in comparison to mutual funds, which are more incentivized to have a larger asset base than to perform well. The divergence in incentives usually results in significant differences in the performances of the two.

Funds of hedge funds

While not the focus of this book, investors who like the notion of diversification may choose to invest in funds of hedge funds. Funds of hedge funds are a diversified portfolio of hedge fund investments in which the fund manager chooses and invests in a number of hedge funds. This blending of different strategies and asset classes aims to provide a more stable long-term investment return than any of the individual funds. The mix of underlying strategies and funds can control returns, risk, and volatility. Capital preservation is generally an important consideration. Volatility depends on the mix and ratio of strategies employed.

Funds of funds charge fees, typically 1 percent of assets under management and 10 percent of any investment gains, to pick hedge funds for clients. The charges come in addition to the 2 percent of assets and 20 percent of gains that go to the underlying hedge funds.

Figure 5: Fund of funds structure

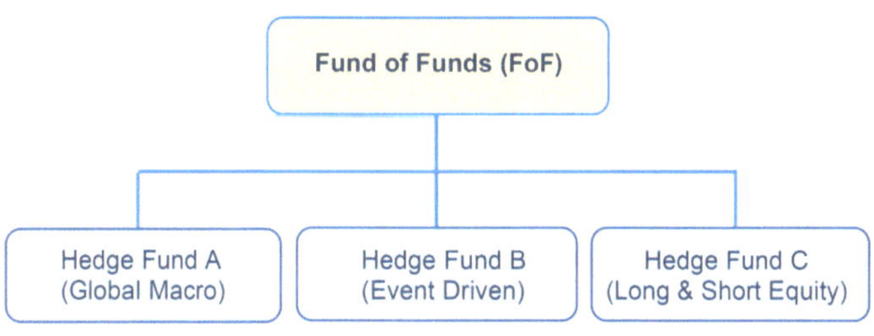

CHAPTER FOUR

Hedge Fund Styles and Themes

Identifying and understanding the characteristics of the many different hedge fund strategies is essential to capitalizing on the various investment opportunities in hedge funds. This is because not all hedge funds are the same—investment returns, volatility, and risks vary enormously among the different hedge fund strategies. Some strategies, which are not correlated to equity markets, are able to deliver consistent returns with extremely low risk of loss, while others may be equally or more volatile than mutual funds.

Broad categories of hedge funds include market directional, corporate restructuring, convergence trading, and opportunistic strategies:

- **Market directional** faces a certain degree of systematic exposure, so the fund is affected by movements in the financial markets, and this category includes long/short equity, emerging markets, activist, managed futures, and short bias.
- **Corporate restructuring** takes profit from such major corporate events, such as bankruptcies or mergers, and includes distressed securities, and merger arbitrage.
- **Convergence trading** takes offsetting positions in two similar securities with disparate prices to profit from a narrowing of the spread between the two securities. This category consists of fixed-income arbitrage, convertible bond arbitrage, equity market-neutral, and relative value arbitrage.

- **Opportunistic strategies** take advantage of any opportunities identified in any marketplace, and include global, macro, and multi-strategy hedge funds.

Each strategy has its own advantages and disadvantages, which depend largely on the investor's perspective. A macro-hedge fund, for example, invests in stocks, bonds, currencies, and other securities from multiple countries to profit from significant shifts in the global or a specific country's economic outlook (i.e., interest rate spikes). It is thus more volatile but potentially faster growing than a distressed-securities hedge fund, which buys the equity or debt of companies that are about to enter or exit financial distress and thus may take months or even years to realize profit.

Table 2: Common hedge fund styles

Style	Description	Expected volatility
Income	Invests with primary focus on yield or current income rather than solely on capital gains. May utilize leverage to buy bonds and sometimes fixed income derivatives in order to profit from principal appreciation and interest income.	Low
Market Neutral-Securities Hedging	Invests equally in long and short equity portfolios generally in the same sectors of the market. Market risk is greatly reduced, but effective stock analysis and stock picking is essential to obtaining meaningful results. Leverage may be used to enhance returns. Usually low or no correlation to the market. Sometimes uses market index futures to hedge out systematic (market) risk. Relative benchmark index usually T-bills.	Low
Market Neutral-Arbitrage	Attempts to hedge out most market risk by taking offsetting positions, often in different securities of the same issuer. For example, can be long convertible bonds and short the underlying issuers equity. May also use futures to hedge out interest rate risk. Focuses on obtaining returns with low or no correlation to both the equity and bond markets. These relative value strategies include fixed income arbitrage, mortgage backed securities, capital structure arbitrage, and closed-end fund arbitrage.	Low
Value	Invests in securities perceived to be selling at deep discounts to their intrinsic or potential worth. Such securities may be out of favor or underfollowed by analyst. Long-term holding, patience, and strong discipline are often required until the ultimate value is recognized by the market.	Low to Moderate
Special Situations	Invests in event-driven situations such as mergers, hostile takeovers, reorganizations, or leveraged buyouts. May involve simultaneous purchase of stock in companies being acquired, and the sale of stock in its acquirer, hoping to profit from the spread between the current market price and the ultimate purchase price of the company. May also utilize derivatives to leverage returns and to hedge out interest rate and/or market risk. Results generally not dependent on direction of market.	Moderate
Market Timing	Allocates assets among different asset classes depending on the manager's view of the economic or market outlook. Portfolio emphasis may swing widely between asset classes. Unpredictability of market movements and the difficulty of timing entry and exit from markets add to the volatility of this strategy.	High
Aggressive Growth	Invests in equities expected to experience acceleration in growth of earnings per share. Generally high P/E ratios, low or no dividends; often smaller and micro-cap stocks which are expected to experience rapid growth. Includes sector specialist funds such as technology, banking, or biotechnology. Hedges by shorting equities where earnings disappointment is expected or by shorting stock indexes. Tends to be "long-biased."	High
Emerging Markets	Invests in equity or debt of emerging (less mature) markets that tend to have higher inflation and volatile growth. Short selling is not permitted in many emerging markets, and, therefore, effective hedging is often not available, although Brady debt can be partially hedged via U.S. Treasury futures and currency markets.	Very High
Short Selling	Sells securities short in anticipation of being able to rebuy them at a future date at a lower price due to the manager's assessment of the overvaluation of the securities, or the market, or in anticipation of earnings disappointments often due to accounting irregularities, new competition, change of management, etc. Often used as a hedge to offset long-only portfolios and by those who feel the market is approaching a bearish cycle.	Very High
Macro	Aims to profit from changes in global economies, typically brought about by shifts in government policy that impact interest rates, in turn affecting currency, stock, and bond markets. Participates in all major markets - equities, bonds, currencies and commodities -- though not always at the same time. Uses leverage and derivatives to accentuate the impact of market moves. Utilizes hedging, but the leveraged directional investments tend to make the largest impact on performance	Very High
Opportunistic	Investment theme changes from strategy to strategy as opportunities arise to profit from events such as IPOs, sudden price changes often caused by an interim earnings disappointment, hostile bids, and other event-driven opportunities. May utilize several of these investing styles at a given time and is not restricted to any particular investment approach or asset class.	Varies
Multi Strategy	Investment approach is diversified by employing various strategies simultaneously to realize short- and long-term gains. Other strategies may include systems trading such as trend following and various diversified technical strategies. This style of investing allows the manager to overweight or underweight different strategies to best capitalize on current investment opportunities.	Varies

Source: CAIA

CHAPTER FIVE

Who Manages Hedge Funds?

The people who own assets, or who serve as fiduciaries for the owners, usually do not have the time, interest, or expertise to manage the assets themselves. So they appoint outside expertise (fund managers) to take on the day-to-day investment control of the assets. Fund managers hold trading authority over the account while trade executions are provided by stockbrokers, bond dealers, and other providers. Most fund managers are highly specialized and trade only within their area of expertise and competitive advantage. Their backgrounds can be very diverse, ranging from investment bankers and financial advisors to successful day traders.

There are focused and specialized hedge fund managers who just offer one hedge fund product. Others may offer a small suite of related hedge fund products that utilize different strategies or markets. For example, the company may have a market-neutral fund, global macro fund, and risk arbitrage fund under the same or different managers within the company. There are also large firms that offer both traditional and alternative investment strategies and large financial groups that offer multiple financial services, such as investment banking, brokerage, investment management, insurance, etc.

Fund managers can manage separate accounts or combined accounts. Separate accounts have only one investor, while combined accounts have two or more investors. The separate account could be a joint account between a married couple (Mr. and Mrs. Lee) and there would be no other outside members invested in that account. In a combined account, Mr. and Mrs. Lee would have to invest alongside Mr. and Mrs. Han.

Most fund management firms have a minimum investment requirement for setting up a separate account. This minimum sum depends on the individual firm's target market. A firm that caters to large institutions could set the minimum as high as $10 million, while a firm that caters to high-net-worth individuals could set the bar as low as $100,000.

CHAPTER SIX

Who Invests in Hedge Funds?

Hedge funds are available to institutional investors like pension funds, endowments, insurance companies, family offices, and private banks. Hedge funds are also available to individual investors who are accredited investors, having met certain requirements (such as a minimum annual income or amount of assets owned) set by their domestic regulatory bodies. These qualifications imply that traditional hedge fund investors understand the investment strategies and risks common to hedge funds. For example, Korea's Financial Services Commission (FSC), Singapore's Monetary Authority of Singapore (MAS), and the UK's Financial Services Authority (FSA) have established regulations that are distinct from one another. Unlike mutual funds, hedge funds are generally not sold to the public or retail investors. For hedge funds that are registered for retail sale, there are still requirements, such as minimum investment sums and the eligibility of investor.

Institutional investors

Institutional investors in hedge funds from developed countries like the U.S., UK, and Japan have typically been pension funds and/or endowment funds that have sufficient capital to diversify their portfolios. There has been an upward trend in investments by institutional investors, with pension funds in the past three years moving toward hedge funds. In fact, it has been projected that investors will allocate about $80 billion more in hedge funds, two thirds of which will come from institutional investors[v].

Consistent with this trend, U.S. pension funds, like the giant $240 billion California Public Employees Retirement System (CalPERS), have picked single hedge fund managers for years to invest 25 percent of their assets, while the $26.3 billion Pennsylvania State Employees' Retirement System has more than 46 percent of its assets in riskier alternatives[vi]. With $110.3 billion under management, Teacher Retirement System of Texas (TRS) is the fifth largest public pension plan in the U.S., and it has declared gains of an average of 17.8 percent annually, compared with the 16.1 percent of its peers, who do not invest in hedge funds. The massive number of baby boomers retiring has created enormous financial strains on U.S. pension systems, which have already been facing a consistent decline of investment returns. As a result, pension funds are investing more and more in hedge funds, in order to achieve the target returns they need. Similarly, by September 2011, retirement systems with more than $1 billion in assets have increased their stakes in real estate, private equity, and hedge funds to 19 percent, up from 10.7 percent in 2007[vii].

From our analysis, the institutional investors from developed economies choose to invest in hedge funds as part of their diversification strategies. Having taken risk into consideration, institutional investors are more concerned with the protection of their investments and consistent asset growth (say about 8–12 percent per annum), rather than a single year's spectacular return of 30 percent followed by -10 percent the subsequent year. Thus, in terms of choosing a hedge fund, these institutional investors are less concerned with abnormally high returns as long as the hedge funds meet the annual returns targets. Consistency is the most important factor.

In Asia, the appetite for hedge funds was decimated after 2008 and has remained moribund ever since. There is just a small handful of ex-Japan ex-Australia institutional investors. Most of the investable wealth lies in the hands of the first or second generation families where the operating business remains in full force and continues to generate high returns on equity (in the 20–30 percent range), making low volatility and low return investments relatively unattractive. In 2012, only 6 percent of the Asian institutions invested in alternative investment spaces, while primarily investing more than 51 percent in equities and real estate[viii]. Diversification and risk mitigation are concepts that have not been fully developed in the strategies of Asian investors.

Individual investors

High-net-worth-individuals (HNWIs) from developed economies like Switzerland and the United States tend to have different characteristics from HNWIs from developing economies like China and India. The HNWIs from the former group have built up their wealth over many decades and consequently have more conservative attitudes toward wealth than that of Asian HNWIs. They are less obsessed with extremely high returns as long as they can have consistently positive returns. Their main objective is to preserve their wealth and not to increase it aggressively. This difference in attitude makes HNWIs from developed countries more understanding of the hedge funds' performance.

On the other hand, HNWIs from Asia tend to have amassed their wealth from their businesses in a very short period of time. Most of their wealth is recent, and they are searching for the best ways to expand their accumulated wealth to make even more money. Their primary objective is to increase wealth (as opposed to preserve it), so their expectations of fund performances are higher. Often, these individual investors from rapidly growing countries like China expect extremely high returns because they are accustomed to exponential growths of around 30–50 percent per year from their businesses.

In short, there are significant differences in how institutional and individual investors invest money around the globe, and these differences affect their expectations of hedge fund performance.

CHAPTER SEVEN

Due-Diligence

If you (as an investor) would like to invest in a hedge fund, to what criteria should you refer? Here are some general due-diligence guidelines for investing in a particular hedge fund.

Due diligence is a disciplined approach to finding the best possible hedge fund manager. It consists of seven phases:

1. **Hedge fund structure review**

    Define how the hedge fund is organized as a business entity, and identify the structure of the hedge fund manager's operations.

2. **Investment strategy review**

    Document the style, target markets, and securities that a manager invests in for the purpose of understanding the manager's investment strategy.

3. **Performance review**

    How long has the fund manager been managing the fund? How persistent is he/she?

4. **Risk assessment**

    Active risk; Short volatility risk; Counterparty risk.

5. **Administrative review**

   Analyze operational issues that may affect the hedge fund manager and the manager's relationship with clients.

6. **Legal review**

   Evaluate the rules that a hedge fund has in place that must be followed by investors.

7. **Checking references**

Table 3: A Checklist for Due-Diligenc

Key questions to understand a hedge fund's investment program:	What is the hedge fund's investment objective? What is the hedge fund manager's investment process? What is the hedge fund manager's competitive advantage?
Understand a hedge fund manager's investment process:	What is the hedge fund manager's investment universe? What is the general investment strategy of the hedge fund? Does the hedge fund manager have a benchmark, and if so, what is it?
Understand a hedge fund's organizational structure:	Where is the hedge fund manager located? What is the organization chart of key personnel? What are the educational backgrounds and prior experiences of the firm's principals? How did the fund manager learn to do short stocks? What relevant hedge fund experience does the hedge fund manager have? What other experiences, qualifications, and registrations does the hedge fund manager have? What are the depths and qualities of the hedge fund manager's corporate business infrastructure? What is the hedge fund firm's capital structure? Is it a viable business?
Review a hedge fund manager's performance:	How long has the hedge fund manager been actively managing a hedge fund? Have the performance results of the fund been persistent over time? Are performance results the same for each hedge fund the manager manages? How are the hedge fund returns presented? Are the hedge fund returns stated gross or net of all fees? How do the risks and returns of the hedge fund product compare to other similar hedge fund products? If the product outperformed other similar products, how was this achieved? For example, was leverage used?
Questions for the risk review phase:	What is the risk level of the hedge fund strategy? What risks are managed by the fund manager? How does the fund manager measure risk? How does the fund manager manage risk? What are the fund's volatility of returns, leverage risk, concentration risk, market risk, and liquidity risk? What has been the fund's maximum draw-down (loss) and in what circumstances did this occur?
Questions for liquidity:	How often can you redeem the hedge fund investment? Does the hedge fund product have any redemption restrictions (i.e., lock-up periods, notice period, redemption fee)?
Questions for the hedge fund's fee structure:	Is the hedge fund's fee structure clearly disclosed? Do you understand the mechanics of the fee structure? What compensation will your financial advisor receive for selling the hedge fund product? Is this compensation consistent with similar products? Do you understand who is being compensated, when and how much?

CHAPTER EIGHT

Fee Structures

Hedge fund managers usually charge both a management fee and a performance fee for their funds.

Management fees are calculated as a percentage of the fund's net asset value and can range from 1 to 4 percent per year. Traditionally, 2 percent has been the standard rate for many funds and still is today. They are usually expressed as an annual percentage but calculated and paid on a monthly, quarterly, or even semiannual basis. Management fees for hedge funds are supposed to cover the operating costs of the manager, whereas the performance fee provides the manager's profits. For large funds, the management fees can be quite substantial, and discounts may be given for large investments.

The performance fee is usually 20 percent of the fund's profits during any year, but there are funds that charge between 10–50 percent. Performance fees are intended to provide an incentive for a manager to perform well. The rationale behind this is that if the fund's performance is attractive enough, investors will be willing to pay this fee. For example, if a hedge fund manager generates a 20 percent return per year, after management fee, the hedge fund manager will collect 4 percent of those profits, leaving the investor with a 16 percent net return.

Almost all hedge fund performance fees include a high water mark, which means that the performance fee only applies to net profits (i.e., profits after losses in previous years have been recovered). For example, if a fund started with $1.5 billion of assets under management

(AUM) and grew to $2 billion after a year, the manager would have charged a performance fee on the $0.5 billion. From then on, the manager can now only charge a performance fee once the fund grows past $2 billion. That is, if the fund falls back to $1.8 billion the next year and recovers to $2 billion in the following year, the manager cannot apply a performance fee for that increase of $0.2 billion.

While this is supposed to prevent hedge fund managers from receiving fees for inconsistent performances, it can also backfire, as a manager will sometimes close a fund that has suffered serious losses and start a new fund rather than attempt to recover the losses over a number of years without a performance fee.

Some hedge funds charge a redemption fee for early withdrawals during a specified period of time (for example, one year) or when withdrawals exceed a predetermined percentage of the original investment. The purpose of the fee is to discourage short-term investing, reduce turnover, and deter withdrawals after periods of poor performance.

CHAPTER NINE

Benefits of Hedge Fund Investments

Consistency of performance

Hedge funds seek to profit from both rising and falling markets and can invest in any asset class or instrument to do so, unlike traditional mutual funds that rely purely on assets gaining in value. This unique capability of hedge funds enables them to deliver consistently high returns, regardless of the overall health of the market.

Low correlation to markets

Given that hedge funds can profit in rising or falling market conditions, they have very different risk/return characteristics from traditional mutual funds. They can be highly adaptable to evolving market trends. This is also beneficial to business owners in sunset industries, as hedge fund investments can serve as an alternative income generator and a form of business diversification.

Wealth preservation and creation

Hedge funds' goal of gaining absolute returns enables them to preserve wealth and creating new wealth through compounding and escaping the negative effects of inflation.

Downside protection

Hedge funds can protect against declining markets by using various hedging strategies. They can also potentially profit from declining markets through short selling and dynamic trading strategies.

Sophistication of strategies

Hedge funds have the ability to access highly specialized strategies not typically available through traditional mutual funds. This includes arbitrage techniques that buy and short sell similar assets for their price differentials, or systematic strategies that allow computers to automate trades based on signals from input models.

CHAPTER TEN

Risks of Hedge Funds

Just as with other types of investments, investing in hedge funds comes with a set of risks. The higher than normal returns hedge funds can offer are offset by a usual corresponding increase in risk. Compared to other forms of investments, hedge funds are less transparent, structured, and regulated, which adds to the risk of investment loss.

Below is a general set of risks found in hedge funds. Do note that this list is not exhaustive and that there are other specific risks not listed here that are unique to different fund strategies and asset types.

Counterparty risk

The risk to each party of a contract that the counterparty will not live up to its contractual obligations, such as the Greece bond crisis that took place in early 2012. This risk can also arise from many sources, such as margin and mortgage trading.

Country risk

The risk that each country has established different regulations (tax policies, investment standards) and that a hedge fund needs to comply with each set of rules. Failure to identify appropriate country risk can be extremely dangerous.

Currency risk

Form of risk that arises when currency rates fluctuate and one has assets or liabilities denominated in foreign currency. If currency exchange rates remain constant over time, there would be no effect, but if the domestic currency strengthens against the foreign currency, then there would be a loss (and vice versa).

Liquidity risk

The risk hedge funds face when they trade in illiquid or thin markets and cannot quickly convert an asset to cash or cash equivalents.

Manager risk

Stems from the management of funds.

- Style drift: Fund manager moving away from his/her area of expertise
- Valuation risk: NAV of investments may be inaccurate
- Capacity risk: Placing too much money into one particular strategy
- Concentration risk: Too much exposure to a particular investment, sector, and trading strategy, etc.
- Leverage risk: Borrowing too much money to trade

Pricing risk

Hedge funds' use of complex financial instruments and over-the-counter trading creates possibilities for error as products are difficult to price.

Process risk

Hedge fund manager-specific risk (idiosyncratic risk) related to the structure of the firm and the firm's operations and processes. A lack of transparency often prevents investors from effectively evaluating process risk.

Systematic risk

The risk that the value of an investment will decrease because of moves in market factors, such as interest rates, recessions, and wars. This cannot be avoided even with diversification.

Transparency risk

This can be both a positive and negative factor, as managers are able to maintain their competitive edge by not revealing their fund management strategies, but then it becomes difficult to pinpoint mistakes when the fund goes belly-up, since there was no accountability. Hedge funds are not required to provide periodic pricing or valuation information to investors. In many cases, the underlying investments are not transparent and are known only to the investment manager.

CHAPTER ELEVEN

Collapse of Hedge Funds

These risks of hedge funds can be easily identified by examining earlier cases of hedge fund failures. Hopefully, analyzing these precedents will help you in the identification and prevention of such mishaps.

Long-Term Capital Management (LTCM)'s blowup

It is arguably the most infamous and disastrous event in the hedge fund industry. A group of distinguished economists (a few of them were Nobel laureates) and Wall Street's top traders founded the LTCM firm in 1994. The fund used mainly fixed-income arbitrage and long/short equity by buying undervalued assets and selling overvalued ones according to their economic models, essentially betting values of the two or more assets converging.

Because of the nature of this type of trading, which only have an expected return of 1 or 2 percent at best, LTCM used leverage to a level the industry never heard of—25:1 in its early days and eventually 100:1 in its peak. The problem arose when LTCM, in 1997, thought that U.S. Treasuries were at a premium over Russian government bonds, so it went long in Russian bonds and shorted Treasuries. However, the Russian financial crisis hit in 1998, causing the two to diverge even as Russian bonds practically became worthless and investors fled to Treasuries, ultimately driving up the price. This forced LTCM to liquidate most of its other positions, causing the firm to lose a total $4.6 billion in matter of months. The bigger problem, however, was its enormous debt from leverage, which was over a $100 billion. The Federal Reserve eventually facilitated a bailout and LTCM closed its fund in 2000.

The Bayou hedge fund fraud

It started as a legitimate hedge fund, but it quickly turned into a fraud after it tried to conceal its losses. The principals established a broker, Bayou Securities, to process the fund's trades. Bayou Securities received commissions from the Bayou Fund and rebated the commissions to conceal the losses. In addition, the Bayou Fund proceeded to fabricate false financial statements. In particular, the managers fired their independent auditors and created an accounting firm by the name of Richmond-Fairfield Associates. This newly created accounting firm created fictitious audit documents verifying the falsified financial statements. Through 2004, the fund continued to operate, falsify records, and solicit additional investor capital. During 2004, all of the fund's assets were transferred to Israel. In 2005, the state of Arizona discovered that large sums of money were being transferred overseas and stumbled onto the fraud.

The Bernie Madoff ponzi scheme

Madoff simply took in investor capital, created fictitious financial reports indicating impressive results, and fulfilled redemption requests from old investors using capital collected from new investors. The accounting firm that served as the independent auditor for Bernie Madoff was not a legitimate operation, and this should have been a major clue to investors. A key lesson from the Madoff case is the importance of performing the proper due diligence on a fund, fund managers, and the independent auditors of the firm.

Lessons from these cases

- Impact of leverage: While significant amounts of leverage can create spectacular returns, it is evident that leverage may also create spectacular collapses as with LTCM. Leverage is a double-edged sword that magnifies both gains and losses.
- Role of banks and prime brokers in the operation of hedge funds: Hedge funds cannot rely on sympathy from banks and prime brokers when trouble occurs. Banks and prime brokers have a responsibility to protect their collateral and are unlikely to offer greater flexibility in times of crisis.
- Importance due diligence plays in hedge fund investing: In the case of Bayou, a little due diligence would have revealed that the independent auditor was in fact a sham.

CHAPTER TWELVE

Famous Hedge Fund Managers

Despite the occasional large-scale failures as mentioned in the previous chapter, hedge funds are typically known to have some of the best performing managers in the investment world. These so-called star managers have gained enormous amounts of both fame and fortune since the early days of the industry.

Some of these earlier figures include:

- *Julian Robertson,* manager of the legendary equity long/short Tiger Funds.
- *George Soros,* whose global-macro Quantum fund earned $1.8 billion in a single week of September 1992 by infamously shorting the British pound.
- *Jim Simons* of Renaissance Technologies, who was one of the first to employ mathematical models and systematic trading to the company's flagship Medallion fund. All three of these managers are still active today, but each spends most of his time managing his own wealth.

Below is a list of some of the recent high-performing hedge fund managers:

Ray Dalio

Bridgewater Associates (Global-Macro)

Though Ray Dalio opened his fund as early as 1973, he has received the most attention in the last five years. His firm, Bridgewater Associates, became largest hedge fund last year, now with more than $120 billion AUM. Bridgewater is a global macro fund with a quantitative approach—the fund is known to implement proprietary models of the markets as well as an innovative portfolio construction. The firm gained over 20 percent in 2011, and Dalio topped the list of highest-paid managers, personally earning $3 billion.

David Einhorn

Greenlight Capital (Long/short Equity)

David Einhorn is one of the younger hedge fund managers who has had a massive influence in equity markets recently. His company, Greenlight Capital, runs primarily an long/short equity strategy but also invests in corporate debt. Einhorn rose to fame in 2008 when he publicly announced his short position in Lehman Brothers during March and was proven to be correct by the end of the year when the company declared bankruptcy. Since then, many investors have followed his short ideas on specific stocks, some of which, notably Green Mountain Coffee Roasters, plunged in a matter of seconds after his speeches.

David E. Shaw

D. E. Shaw & Co. (Systematic and Computer-Driven)

David Shaw was a former faculty member in the computer science department at Columbia University before he established his company D. E. Shaw, one of the most famous and successful quantitative hedge funds in history. The company currently has $26 billion AUM, making it one of the ten biggest hedge funds in the United States. Shaw's success stands as he employed quantitative and technological approaches when such were still largely unfamiliar in the investment community. Almost all of the company's trades are automated based on the signals that Shaw's proprietary mathematical and computer models give, and thus a significant part of the company is devoted to research and development of such models.

Bill Ackman

Pershing Square Capital Management (Activist Investing)
Bill Ackman is a famous value investor who runs a concentrated portfolio using an activist strategy. Ackman focuses on companies with low debt whose stock prices temporarily drop in the markets. He exercises his influence on the board using these shares to increase shareholder value, usually through selling parts of the company's assets and spinning off its branches to raise cash. Some of his most famous cases are with Borders Group, JC Penney, and Canadian Pacific Railway.

CHAPTER THIRTEEN

Regulatory Overview of Hedge Funds

Because of the subprime mortgage crisis in 2006, financial crisis in 2008, and the European debt crisis in 2008–12, the hedge fund industry has faced drastic changes and measures that have limited its autonomy, despite the general consensus that hedge funds had little contribution toward the financial crises. Some of the key regulatory changes in the industry are identified below:

United States

Form PF

New rule adopted by the Securities and Exchange Commission (SEC) and Commodity Futures Trading Commission (CFTC) that requires private fund advisors to file disclosure data on holdings and risk exposures within their funds. SEC requires private funds with more than $5 billion in regulatory assets under management to submit their initial filings after the second quarter of 2012. Firms with regulatory assets under management greater than $150 million will be required to file in early 2013.

Private fund clients must also synthesize the holdings data required for Form PF with risk calculations, which are often generated by third parties other than the fund administrator. The SEC will evaluate how risk data provided in Form PF matches risk data supplied to investors, to ensure that risk reporting is consistent across functions.

FACTA issues for hedge funds

The U.S. Foreign Account Tax Compliance Act (FATCA) imposes a 30 percent withholding tax on U.S. persons holding offshore accounts on certain "withholdable payments" to "foreign financial institutions," which do not provide information about their U.S. accounts to the Internal Revenue Service. Section 102 of the bill expands the definition of a foreign financial institution to include entities that engage in derivative transactions (hedge funds). Additionally, Sections 203 and 204 of the bill imposes anti-money laundering requirements on unregistered investment companies, including hedge funds and private equity funds, and formation agents. Hedge funds are required to establish AML programs; ascertain the identity of investors, including beneficial owners of foreign entities; and submit suspicious activity reports. Agents engaged in the business of forming corporations or other legal entities would also be required to establish AML programs.

Large trader reporting

The new Rule 13h–1 requires certain large traders to provide information regarding their trading activities to the SEC. A "large trader" is defined as a person whose transactions in exchange-listed securities equal or exceed two million shares or $20 million during any calendar day, or twenty million shares or $200 million during any calendar month[ix]. This will enhance the agent's ability to identify large market participants, collect information on trading, and analyze their trading activity. It imposes record keeping, reporting, and limited monitoring requirements on certain registered broker-dealers through whom large traders execute their transactions.

New definitions

The definition of an "accredited investor" has changed. The term used to include the value of house in net worth, but now it excludes its value in calculating net worth[x].

In general, all of the regulatory changes increase the reporting requirements of investment advisors and limit the ability of these advisors to exclude information in reporting to the various federal government agencies. They are not favorable to the hedge fund space since they would significantly limit hedge funds' autonomy and disclose the hedge funds' secretive nature to the public; and hedge funds would suffer from additional costs to conform with the new regulations.

JOBS Act

On top of these regulatory changes in the United States, the JOBS Act could affect the marketing and promotion of hedge funds, presentation of performance metrics, and creative avenues for managers to raise AUM. The JOBS Act will not go into effect until the SEC completes the formal process of drafting and approving the new regulations, which is supposed to be ninety days from April 5, 2012. However, this deadline could be extended.

The JOBS Act removes the general solicitation and general advertising prohibition for "rule 506 exempt private offerings," which is the regulatory framework under which most hedge funds now operate. Previously, hedge funds could not engage in any act of general advertising or general solicitation. Because of the restrictions, hedge fund managers could only discuss their fund with a very close and restricted group of potential investors. This made it very difficult for new managers to build their businesses and raise enough capital. With the new regulations under the JOBS Act, however, these restrictions on capital-raising will be rendered obsolete. As a result, private fund managers will have a broad array of capital-raising options that were previously not given to them. Managers will be able to engage in advertising, media broadcasts, public websites, interviews, social media, e-mail campaigns, and any number of other marketing strategies to generate interest in their fund.

Managers still cannot engage in anything that that would be deemed manipulative or deceptive advertising by regulators. There are specific ways that investment managers need to structure and phrase performance advertising.

- The effect of material market or economic conditions must be disclosed
- Managers cannot use "cherry-picking" when presenting returns
- Results must show the deduction of fees and expenses
- Managers cannot make claims about profits without also disclosing the possibility of loss

Another key point to consider is that the rule 506 prohibition on general advertising will be removed if all investors in the fund are accredited. Formerly, you could have up to thirty-five non-accredited investors in a hedge fund. In addition, a manger used to rely on an investor's claim to be an accredited investor, but now the burden of proof falls on the manager's shoulders to perform adequate due-diligence to ensure that his investors are accredited. The management company itself will have to certify that the investor is accredited.

Europe

The latest regulations have put Europe on the path toward the most heavily regulated hedge fund industry. In spite of that, 95 percent of investors interviewed by *Preqin* anticipate little to no effect on hedge fund portfolios[xi].

The Alternative Investment Fund Managers Directive (AIFMD)

AIFMD was proposed in response to the 2008 global financial crisis. It is set to be implemented in July 2013 with the goals of increasing transparency, improving investor protection, and safeguarding the financial system. This directive will affect how alternative hedge fund managers distribute funds, compensate employees, and structure businesses. In other words, there will be more governmental oversight and incurred costs. However, European Commission still has to clarify key issues and provisions regarding the new directive.

The Markets in Financial Instruments Directive (MiFID II)

MiFID II was proposed in 2007. It has since been implemented in Ireland and will be enforced in the European Economic Area (EEA) beginning in 2014. The provisions will also seek to increase transparency, but with a greater focus on specific business practices and regulations after financial crisis.

Solvency II

Proposed in 2009, it was to be implemented in 2013 but has since been delayed to 2014. As a supplement to the previously mentioned regulations, it reviews and updates minimum required capital levels by giving leeway for companies to choose their own risk profiles and match them with appropriate capital levels in order to better identify risks and mitigation process.

In addition, European hedge funds operating in the United States are subject to U.S. regulations, such as the U.S. Dodd-Frank Wall Street Reform and Consumer Protection Act and the U.S. Foreign Account Tax Compliance Act.

Singapore

Recent regulations in Singapore have been changed to the following conditions:

Hedge fund managers with less than S $250 million and with less than thirty qualified investors are exempt from the licensing requirement. However, they are required to maintain a base capital of at least S $250,000 and notify the Monetary Authority of Singapore (MAS) about their business. Hedge fund firms in Singapore that manage more than S $250 million (US $183 million) will need to be licensed.

Fund management companies that serve accredited or institutional investors must be licensed. They are required to maintain a base capital of at least S $250,000. Similarly, fund management firms that serve retail investors and/or manage a larger portfolio of assets must be licensed. The base capital requirement varies from S $500,000 to S $1,000,000.

Fund management firms must maintain customers' monies and assets with independent custodians, ensuring segregation of duties between the functions of fund management and fund administration. All fund managers will be subject to the same requirements for business conduct.

Hong Kong

Similarly, Hong Kong has updated its hedge fund regulations to the following terms:

The hedge fund manager should apply for the appropriate license from the Securities and Futures Commission of Hong Kong (SFC) and prove it has a proper business structure, internal control systems, and qualified personnel. A hedge fund authorized by the SFC is eligible to offer their services to the public, while an unregulated hedge fund can only offer their services to those who qualify as professional investors.

The minimum regulatory capital required for a hedge fund manager varies depending on the licensing conditions and type of activities that he or she is approve to carry on. There is a general prohibition on the marketing of non-SFC-authorized hedge funds (regardless of its place of domicile) in Hong Kong, unless the marketing efforts are made only to professional investors.

If the hedge fund is an SFC-authorized hedge fund, the SFC must authorize the promotional material before it can be released to the public. If the hedge fund is a single hedge fund (that is, not a fund of hedge funds), there is no strict limitation on the investment direction, types of financial instruments in which the fund can invest in, diversification, concentration of investments, or strategies and the extent and basis of leverage. However, the fund must clearly define these conditions in the fund's constitutive and offering documents. In respect to an authorized fund of hedge funds, the fund must invest in at least five underlying funds, and not more than 30 percent of the fund's total net asset value can be invested in any one of the underlying funds. The fund also cannot invest in another fund of hedge funds.

The manager of an SFC-authorized hedge fund is required to issue regular reports to its investors at least on a quarterly basis. There is no restriction on the minimum or maximum number of investors in a hedge fund. The minimum level of initial subscription by each investor of an SFC-authorized hedge fund should not be less than US $50,000 equivalent, except for fund of funds, where the minimum initial subscription should not be less than US $10,000 equivalent. No minimum subscription level will apply to a hedge fund which provides at least 100 percent capital guarantee. There is no minimum or maximum subscription level on follow-on investments by investors.

Cayman Islands

Previously, master funds were exempt from the registration and reporting obligations imposed on other Cayman-based mutual funds, which applied to mutual funds with fifteen or fewer investors. The new provisions mean that certain mutual funds previously exempt under that provision will now be deemed as master funds and will be required to register with the Cayman Islands Monetary Authority (CIMA) if they have one or more Cayman-based, regulated feeder funds as an investor. A feeder fund is a mutual fund that conducts more than 51 percent of its investing through another mutual fund.

There are no prohibitive licensing and regulatory provisions calling for local custodians, managers or directors. There are also no restrictions placed on investment objectives, risks, rates of return, leveraging or other commercial matters given the institutional and sophisticated nature of the investors in Cayman hedge funds or mutual funds. The law requires that the offering memorandum describes comprehensively the equity interests and contains sufficient information (on objectives, risks, service providers, conflicts of interest, etc.) to enable the investor to make an informed decision.

A regulated investment fund must qualify under the law before starting business. To do so, it may either obtain its own license, appoint a licensed mutual fund administrator in the Cayman Islands to provide its principal office, or be automatically registered if it is for a sophisticated investor. For example, the minimum investment per investor is US $100,000. Funds established before November 14, 2006 are permitted to retain the previous minimum investment requirement of US $50,000. Registered mutual funds are suitable for funds with a minimum subscription of US $100,000.

British Virgin Islands

Starting on January 1, 2011, all funds had to comply with the requirements of the Securities and Investment Business Act, 2010 (SIBA) instead of the current Mutual Funds Act of 1996 (MFA). The new laws are much stricter than the previous laws and continue the push by the

BVI Financial Services Commission (FSC) to maintain greater oversight of funds located in the BVI.

Below is an overview of the major new requirements under SIBA:

- Disclaimer on offering documents: in the event a fund offers interests or shares on or after December 31, 2010, the fund offering documents must be amended to include the prescribed investment warning under the new law.
- The subscription agreements must also include an acknowledgment from any new investor that it has received, understood, and accepted the investment warning (note: these documents must be filed with the Financial Services Commission within fourteen days of their issue).
- All private funds must at all times have at least two directors (at least one of which is an individual) and must have a manager, an administrator, and a custodian who is independent from the manager and administrator. Appointing a new custodian, administrator, prime broker, or manager must be reported to the commission at least seven days *prior* to the appointment.

In sum, there are no restrictions on the investment policies and strategies of a mutual fund in Cayman or the BVI and no legal restrictions on its power to borrow, other than those specifically contained in the fund's prospectus or its constitutional documents. There are no restrictions on the arrangements which a Cayman or BVI fund may wish to make with respect to prime brokers.

Malta

Maltese funds are regulated by the MFSA under The Investment Services Act 1994 (and later revisions). There are several different types of collective investment schemes or funds that can be registered in Malta, each suited to different sorts of funds or levels of investment. Collective investment schemes in Malta can be set up under a number of legal structures: a collective investment company with fixed or variable share capital; a unit trust; a mutual fund; or a limited partnership.

The fund itself usually takes one of two forms: either a professional investor fund (PIF) or a private scheme. Private schemes are those that have no more than fifteen participants. The regulator must ascertain that the participants are all closely associated with the promoters and that the fund is essentially private in nature and purpose. PIFs are open to extraordinary investors, qualifying investors, or experienced investors, depending on the minimum investment and net assets of the investors. Extraordinary investors must have assets of over €7.5 million and qualifying investors over €750,000. Experienced investors must have the knowledge and experience to be able to make their own decisions regarding investment and recognize the risks involved. Experienced investor funds require an initial minimum investment of €15,000. However, many funds impose a minimum investment limit of €100,000 in order to avoid the more retail end of the market.

PIFs offer low setup costs and tax-saving advantages. Funds based in Malta are exempt from income and capital gains tax. For funds where less than 85 percent of their assets are situated in Malta, no withholding tax is imposed on investment income.

The main advantages of Malta as a fund domicile are the following:

1. The level of costs involved (registration and licensing fees as well as professional and service fees) is significantly lower than other fund jurisdictions (e.g., Luxembourg and Ireland).
2. PIFs may be self-managed without the need to appoint a third-party manager. The management of the fund would be undertaken by an investment committee. Self-managed funds are subject to ad hoc rules regarding composition of board members and investment committee, as well as share capital requirements

3. Contrary to other fund jurisdictions, PIFs do not need to appoint a manager, custodian, administrator, or any other service provider who is licensed in or who has otherwise exercised passport rights into Malta (where all underlying investments will be held abroad and the respective services will be provided from outside Malta). The MFSA shall accept any service provider licensed in a recognized jurisdiction for this purpose, including EU/EEA States and jurisdictions with which the local regulator has entered into bilateral or multilateral memoranda of understanding. This allows clients significant flexibility, enabling them to continue using the services of any external service provider licensed in any such jurisdiction with whom they might already have a professional history, and it facilitates the re-domiciliation of offshore funds. A slight exception to this rule is afforded with regard to PIFs' targeting extraordinary investors, where a custodian (for safekeeping arrangements and compliance with the investment objectives of the fund) is rendered necessary. Nevertheless, if clients wish to make use of local service providers, Malta does have the necessary human resources to adequately provide fund-specific services with a number of reputable and licensed service providers.

4. Low qualification entry levels for professional investors with the exception of self-managed funds (where a share capital of € 125,000 is required).

5. Favorable tax regimes.

6. The fund may invest in the underlying assets itself, or through special purpose vehicles (SPVs), local or foreign, which act as the lunga manus for the fund. The use of SPVs may be particularly useful for tax planning by enabling the fund to reap full benefit of the extensive network of double tax treaties (Malta has signed double tax treaties with over fifty jurisdictions).

7. Licensing applications are processed quickly and efficiently. Provided all due diligence documents are submitted to the MFSA, the authority shall issue an "in principal" approval to the proposed promoters of the fund within seven (seven) working days

Tax policies for Malta are as follows:

Collective investment schemes
- Maltese-licensed collective investment schemes may be set up in various forms: corporate, unit trust, partnership.
- Maltese-licensed funds investing outside Malta are tax-exempt.
- No tax is charged on distribution of profits to non-resident share/unit holders.
- Gains on share/unit transfers by non-residents normally exempt.
- No capital/stamp duty on issues/units and exemption available on transfers of shares/units in licensed funds.
- No net asset value tax or other taxes on fund assets.

CHAPTER FOURTEEN

The U.S. Hedge Fund Industry

The birth of the first modern hedge fund is usually credited to the American financial journalist Alfred W. Jones, who, in the 1950s, applied the concept of leverage, equity hedging with short selling, and performance fees to his investors. Since then, hedge funds have grown into Europe and are now emerging in Asia. However, the United States is still regarded as the traditional home of the hedge fund industry.

Industry overview

In 1990, the estimated AUM in hedge funds in the United States was around $40 billion—that number grew to about $500 billion by 2000. As of the end of 2011, the industry now manages roughly over two-thirds of the global hedge fund AUM at $1.3 trillion, a growth of nearly four times in ten years. The graph below also shows that the 2008 crisis significantly cut its assets by $400 billion, during which the industry faced a large net asset draw, but has grown back to its previous size in the following years.

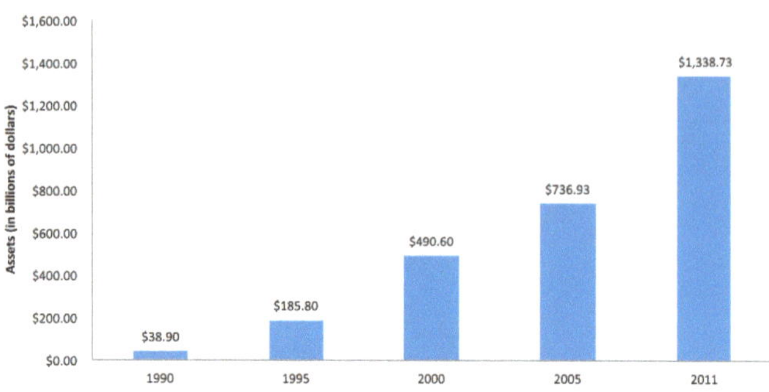

The industry is extremely diverse in terms of AUM per manager, ranging from a few million to over billions of dollars. The graph below shows that smaller firms and only few big players populate the industry. The relatively loose restrictions on hedge funds allow many individuals to run a small sum of money (usually from family/friends and their own pockets), whereas institutions (sources of bigger capital) typically invest in managers already established in managing large sums of assets.

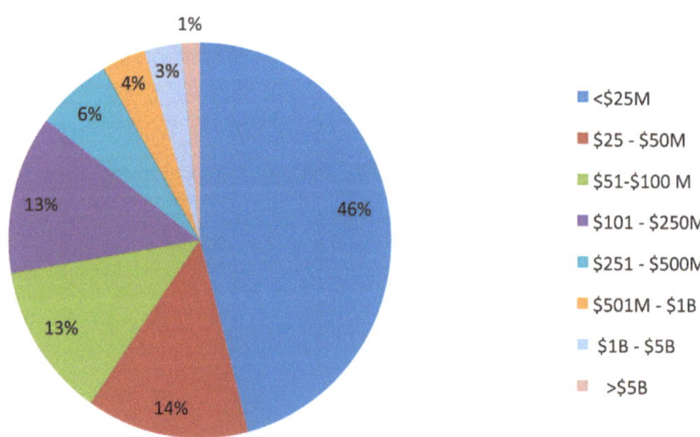

Strategy composition

In the United States, hedge fund strategies have been like fashion objects—different market conditions and the prominence of star managers during different time periods have given rise to trends in the strategies themselves. The chart below shows the estimated strategy composition by AUM in 1990. As it implies, the 1990s are often referred to as the age of the macro-hedge funds, during which the number of macro funds substantially increased, as many of them sought to follow the success of George Soros and Paul Tudor Jones.

Figure 8: Style Composition by AUM-1990

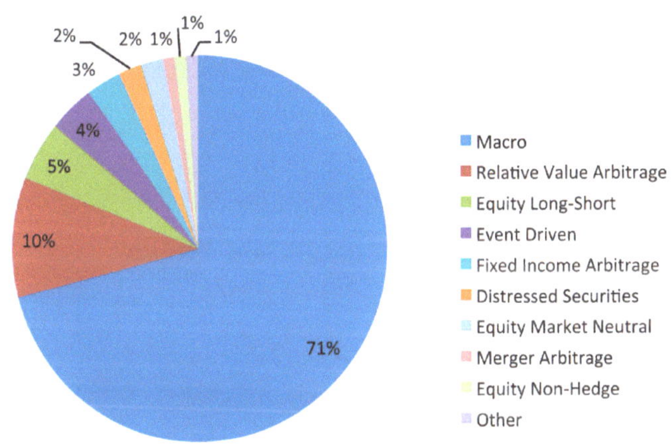

Source: Hedge Fund Research

Much changed in the next decade. The figure below first shows that the market shares of each strategy became more diversified than previously. Long/short equity and other equity-oriented funds managed the most assets as the dot-com bubble led the stock market to new highs.

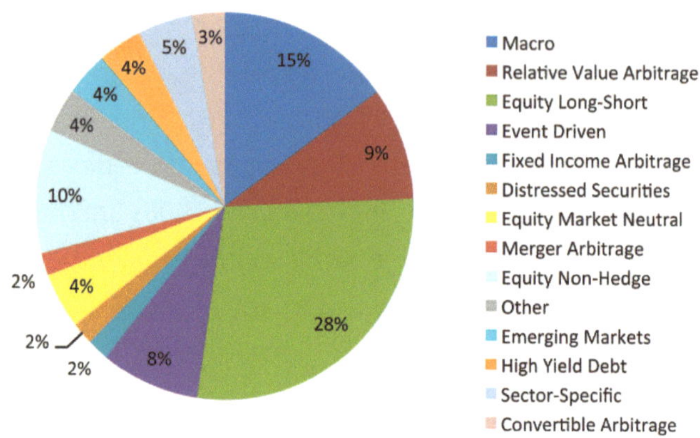

Figure 9: Style Composition by AUM-2000

Source: Hedge Fund Research

The chart below shows the current shape of the hedge fund industry. We can see that there is almost an equal division of assets among each of the four broad strategies. The growth of relative value funds can be accounted by the higher inflow of capital to these funds as fearful investors sought small but consistent absolute returns after the 2008 crisis, while event-driven managers also rose to take advantage of the numerous corporate events in recent years.

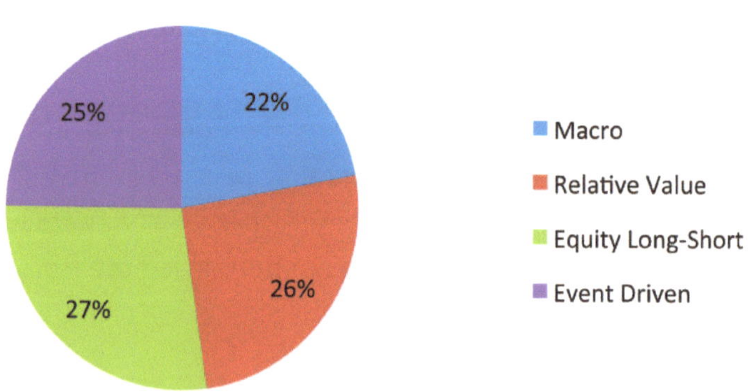

Figure 10: Style Composition by AUM-2011

Source: Hedge Fund Research

Investor profile

One of the most important factors for the tremendous recent growth of the U.S. hedge fund market is the shift of investor type during the last ten years. Hedge funds have traditionally been the investment preference for high-net-worth individuals because of the general public's lack of knowledge regarding them, as well as the managers' preferences to stay under cover. Recently, especially after the 2008 crisis, both the public and traditional asset managers have turned their attention to alternative investments that provide low correlation with the market, and hedge funds naturally caught the media's attention.

As the chart below shows, the distribution of hedge fund investors has shifted heavily toward the so-called institutional investors, who invest much larger sums of capital compared to that of individuals. Foundations refer to public charities and academic/cultural endowments, while corporations include asset managers, insurance companies, and banks.

Figure 11: Investor Distribution by AUM

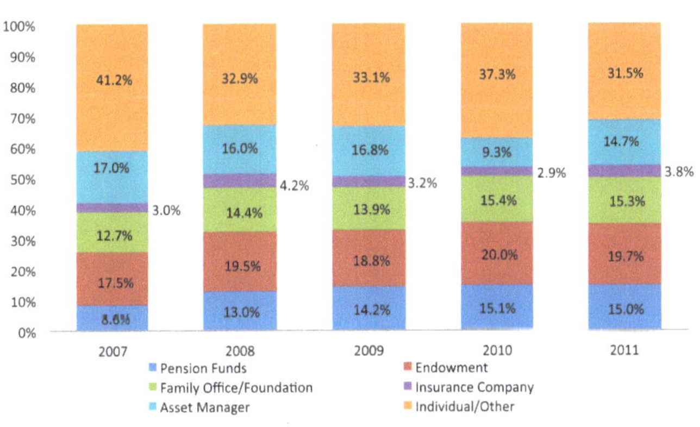

Source: Preqin

Fee structures

The standard has been the 2–20 structure, but much has changed since the 2008 crisis when the industry observed its biggest loss. The two charts below show the distribution of management and performance fees managers employed from 2009 to 2011, in terms of the number of funds. As one would expect, managers cut their management fees and many of them currently charge less than 2 percent to investors. However, performance fees have stayed relatively constant, and in fact more managers started to charge higher than 20 percent. This is because managers who performed well despite the crisis were able to charge higher fees the following years as more investors wished to invest in these specific hedge funds.

Figure 12: Management Fee Distribution by Number of Funds

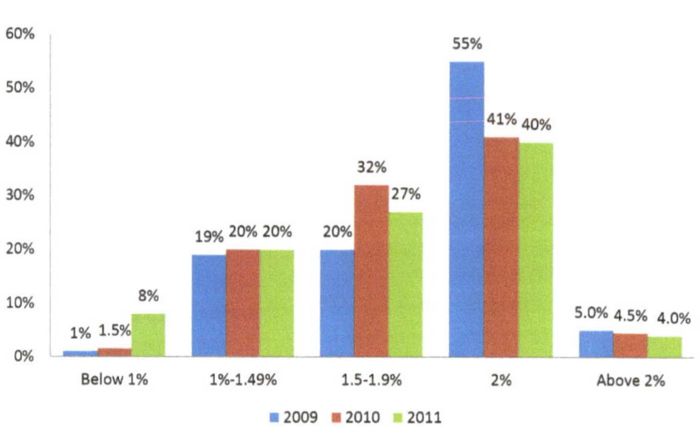

Source: Hedge Fund Research

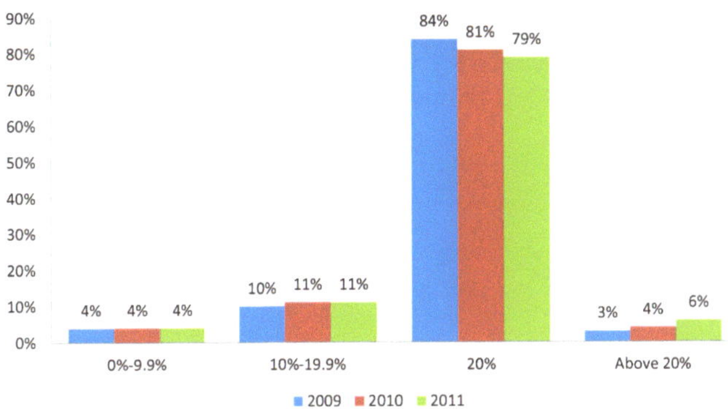

Source: Hedge Fund Research

CHAPTER FIFTEEN

European Hedge Fund Industry

The European hedge fund industry has been subject to some of the greatest changes in the last ten years. It reached the greatest AUM levels at the end of 2007 but lost its steam since the global financial crisis in 2008 and the ensuing Eurozone sovereign debt crisis. Despite signs of recovery in early 2012, the financial situation in Europe still remains bleak. However, compared to other asset classes, the hedge fund industry remains stable, and there are signs of continual growth as European investors indicate unfulfilled target allocations. In light of recent events, hedge funds have been able to uphold a relatively credible and untarnished image, because they were able to preserve wealth without having to resort to financial bailouts.

Industry overview

Europe is the second largest center for fund managers second to the United States. The two core centers for hedge fund activity are in the United Kingdom (UK) and Switzerland. While the UK tends to be more diversified by investor types, consisting of fund of funds, pension funds, endowments, and family offices, Switzerland is dominated by a strong institutional investor base; 70 percent of the European hedge fund assets, totaling $395 billion were managed outside of London.

Since the beginning of 2000, the European hedge fund AUM has grown nearly twelve times—from about $50 billion to the peak of $472 billion in October 2007. However, AUM funds dropped nearly 80 percent in January 2008 because of portfolio losses and redemptions by investors during the global financial crisis. In 2009, there were strong returns on investment, and this positive trend has continued to around $400 billion AUM as of April 2011[xii].

Strategy composition

Currently, investors have been trending toward more direct hedge fund investments over fund of funds. In addition, they seek managers with increased transparency and reduced fees during precarious financial times. In response to the Eurozone crisis, investors are opting to invest in more liquid markets, such as the United States and Japan, and diversify their portfolios by tapping into new sources of alpha.

Investor profile

Since 2007, as the chart below demonstrates, the AUM size of European foundations have been consistently on the increase, indicating that more and more foundations are choosing hedge funds over other investment options. While family offices and asset managers make up the bulk of AUM, pension funds have been increasing over the past two years.

Figure 14: Investor Distribution by AUM

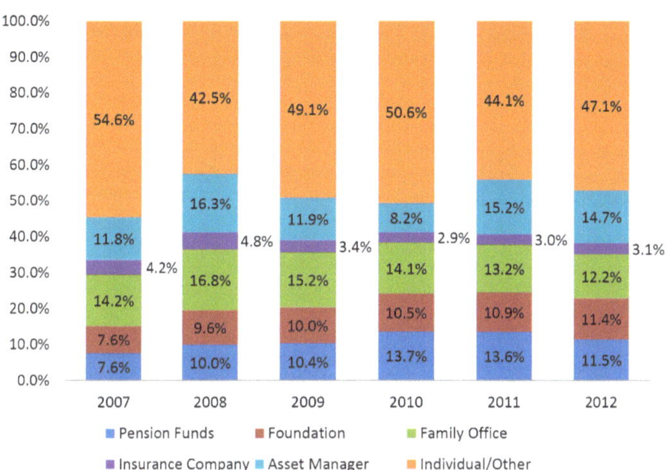

Source: Preqin

CHAPTER SIXTEEN

Asian Hedge Fund Industry

The hedge fund industry in Asia has great potential for exponential growth in asset size and number of hedge funds. Many investors are looking to Asia as a great way to diversify portfolios, especially non-equity correlated investments. Strong, growing economies spearheaded by China are renewing economic recovery and growth. However, as mentioned in chapter six, HNWIs, or individual investors, from Asia tend to have different approaches to investments than those from developed economies. While the U.S. and European investors are intent on preserving wealth, investors from Asia tend to expect high fund performances in order to aggressively increase their wealth.

Industry overview

The Asian hedge fund industry has an AUM size of US $124.1 billion, as of January 2012. This industry has grown nearly twenty-two times since 1996, reaching AUM levels of US $5.5 million, but it has failed to regain the 2007 peak AUM level of US $176 billion[xiii]. With the top 20 percent of hedge fund managers managing 80 percent of total assets in Asia, clearly big hedge fund firms dominate the region. However, there are still many mid-size hedge funds being launched. In 2011, there was a 60 percent increase in new hedge funds[xiv].

Currently China serves as the most popular location for hedge fund firms investing in Asia. Accounting for 30 percent of hedge funds globally, China ranks as the leading location within Asia, and fourth globally. China is also expected to emerge as the greatest source of capital for hedge funds in the Asia markets. This growth will propel peripheral cities, where hedge funds tend to be located, such as Hong Kong, Shanghai, and Singapore, to global prominence[xv]. The growth and diversification of capital markets has transformed Asia into a viable center for investors. Furthermore, the rather undeveloped nature of hedge funds enables strategic hedge fund investors to take advantage of price anomalies and achieve competitive return rates.

Strategy composition

There is a strong preference for long and short equity strategies, which dominate 76 percent of hedge funds in Asia, compared with 46 percent in the global industry as of January 2011. This can be explained by the strict regulations by countries on capital accounts with only four liberalized currencies: Japan, Australia, Hong Kong, and Singapore. Only currency and rates can compete as a type of uncorrelated alternative to equities. The next category is diversified, event driven, or relative value. Finally, global macro strategies are used, but they make up only 5 percent of the hedge funds, compared with 22 percent globally. In addition, Asian managers tend to fixate on local currencies and rates instead of engaging in wider global markets[xvi].

CHAPTER SEVENTEEN

A Growing Industry—Hedge Funds in Korea

This chapter is designed to introduce the newly born hedge fund industry in South Korea. South Korea officially allowed the creation of hedge funds on December 23, 2011. As of today, there are nineteen hedge funds, each with an asset size ranging from US $3 to $120 million. Total assets under management (AUM) as of August 2012 was 717.9 billion KRW, which is approximately US $633 million[xvii].

Background on short selling policies

As mentioned throughout this book, short selling is an essential tool for hedge funds in order to seek absolute returns even in bear markets. Naked short selling or short selling without borrowing the securities first, is strictly prohibited under Korean law, although covered short selling is allowed by both institutional and retail investors. However, regulators decide on the list of stocks, bonds, or other assets that can be put up for short selling, and licensed securities companies are allowed to lend these upon availability. For example, Korean regulators have banned short selling of any form on all financial stocks. Furthermore, on March 2012, the Korean Financial Services Commission (FSC) announced that by the end of 2012, regulations will be enforced so that investors will be required to report their short positions if they exceed a certain designated quantity.

Regulations on hedge funds and their investors

- Where Hedge Funds Fit in Under the Law
  Hedge funds are grouped as a special branch under private equity funds under regulations termed, "Professional Private Equity Funds." They are, however, exempt from most asset allocation rules that traditional private equity funds face (for example, all private equity funds in Korea must invest at least 50 percent of their capital in domestic distressed companies) and are free to trade all types of securities and derivatives.
- Establishing a Hedge Fund
  The fund's parent company must hold at least 1 trillion KRW if it is a securities company, or 10 trillion KRW (around US $8.6 billion) if it is an asset/investment management company in AUM. It must also have at least 6 billion KRW in paid-in-capital and three managers or more with a defined track past record. Leverage is capped at 400 percent. This is higher than the initial intended rate of 300 percent, because policymakers are loosening up regulations to grow the industry.
- Investing in Hedge Funds
  The minimum investment is 500 million KRW, and this is the same requirement for retail investors. Unlike the United States, there is no further net-worth requirement for individual investors. The logic is that as the top 1 percent of the income distribution in Korea have an average net worth of 3.1 billion KRW (while the top 5 percent, 1.3 billion KRW), only these individuals can afford to invest this sum. The minimum was initially intended to be 1 billion KRW, but again policymakers have lowered the doors to increase demand.

Characteristics of Korean hedge funds

Due to relatively higher entrance barriers to start a fund, the trend has been for traditional, large asset management companies to provide hedge funds as one of their many products. Fee structures are similar but generally lower than that of the United States, with management fees ranging from 0.3 to 1 percent and performance fees from 10–20 percent. One interesting fact is that only three of these funds employ a high water mark system. The rest apply a performance fee to gains over an absolute benchmark rate specified at the fund's inception, the rate ranging from 4 to 8 percent annually.

The Korean investment community, however, has not been too optimistic about these hedge funds, as they are unfamiliar with the concept and the higher fees compared to those of mutual funds. Raising capital has thus been more difficult for these hedge funds than expected. Therefore, a bulk of the starting capital for these funds comes from the management company's in-house financial affiliates, while the rest comes from its prime brokers and some retail investors.

Because of this tendency for capital to rotate under the bigger umbrella company, funds are also sold by sister financial branches. They are usually securities companies that already have a base of high-net-worth clients. To highlight, Samsung Investment Management, which has the largest retail investor base (54 billion KRW), raised this capital through Samsung Securities, who is also its biggest investor and prime broker.

Prime brokerage

For a firm to be qualified as a prime broker for a hedge fund in Korea, it must hold at least 3 trillion KRW in equity capital. This severely limits the number of possibilities for a handful of domestic firms. However, regulators are also enforcing boundaries to limit foreign investment banks from entering the business.

Currently there are five institutions licensed to provide prime-brokerage services. These include Hyundai Securities, KDB Daewoo Securities, Woori Securities, Hangook Securities, and Samsung Securities. Of these, Daewoo has the biggest market share at 52 percent, and the others are illustrated below.

Figure 15: Market Share of Prime Brokers in Korea, by AUM

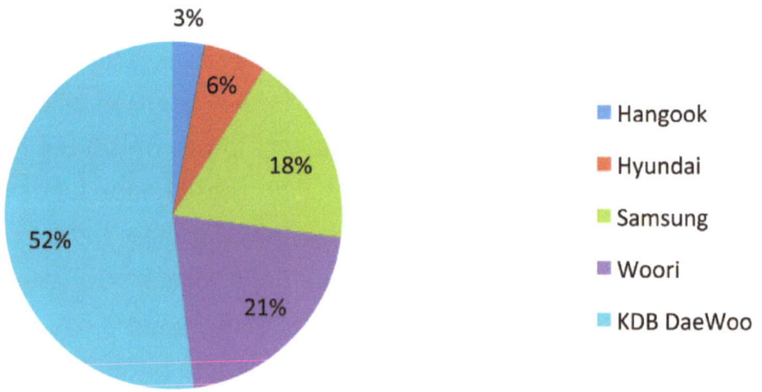

Source: Chosun Biz

Current performances

The following page shows the summary of the hedge funds and their performances since inception. The relatively poor performance has been a result of the exceptional performance of the KOSPI index, causing many of the funds' short positions to erase the gains of the long ones. However, one must note that three to five months is an extremely short period of time to evaluate a manager's performance.

Table 4 shows that Mirae Assets and Samsung manage around half of the capital invested in hedge funds. We can also see from Figure 4 that two-thirds of the total assets are managed in long/short equity funds, primarily because they are offered the most. Mirae Assets' Smart Q Total Return fund, the only fixed-income arbitrage fund in the industry, is the largest with its AUM accounting for almost a fourth of the industry.

Table 4: Summary of Korea's Hedge Funds
Note: Returns are as of May 8, 2012

Company Name	Inception Date	Fund Name	AUM (billion KRW)	Style	Total Return (%)
DongYang	16-Dec-11	DongYang My Ace Low-Risk	4.1	Equity Long-Short (domestic)	-3.27
	16-Dec-11	DongYang My Ace Middle-Risk	16.9	Equity Long-Short (domestic)	-0.79
Mirae Asset Investments	16-Dec-11	Mirae Asset Egis Long-Short	14.9	Equity Long-Short (domestic/global)	-0.5
Mirae Asset MAPS	16-Dec-11	Mirae Asset Smart Q Opportunity	14.9	Equity Long-Short (domestic/global)	2.4
	16-Dec-11	Mirae Asset Smart Q Total Return	137.1	Fixed Income Arbitrage	2.49
Samsung Investment	16-Dec-11	Samsung H Club Equity Hedge	83.2	Equity Long-Short (domestic/global)	5.08
	17-Dec-11	Samsung H Club Multi-Strategy	38.6	Multi-Strategy	0.69
ShinHan – BNP Paribas	16-Dec-11	ShinHan-BNP Domestic Equity Long-Short	56.9	Equity Long-Short (domestic)	-3.04
	16-Dec-11	ShinHan BNP Asia ex-Japan Equity Long-Short	29	Equity Long-Short (domestic/global)	-4.24
Woori Investment	16-Dec-11	Woori Heritage Long-Short	10.1	Equity Long-Short (domestic)	0.42
Hana-UBS	19-Dec-11	Hana-UBS Prime Long-Short Alpha	25.1	Equity Long-Short (domestic)	1.09
Hangook Investment	16-Dec-11	Hangook Investment Fundamental Long-Short	30	Equity Long-Short (domestic/global)	-3.43
Hanhwa	16-Dec-11	Hanhwa Asia Pacific Long-Short	20	Equity Long-Short (domestic/global)	-5.12
KDB Investment	3-Feb-12	KDB Pioneer Long-Short Neutral	30	Equity Long-Short (domestic/global)	-7.89
	3-Feb-12	KDB Pioneer Long-Short Low Risk	12.5	Equity Long-Short (domestic/global)	-3.39
Kyobo AXA	27-Feb-12	Kyobo Magnum 1	22	Multi-Strategy	-0.84
KB	13-Jan-12	KB K-Alpha	30	Equity Long-Short	3.19

Source: Chosun Biz

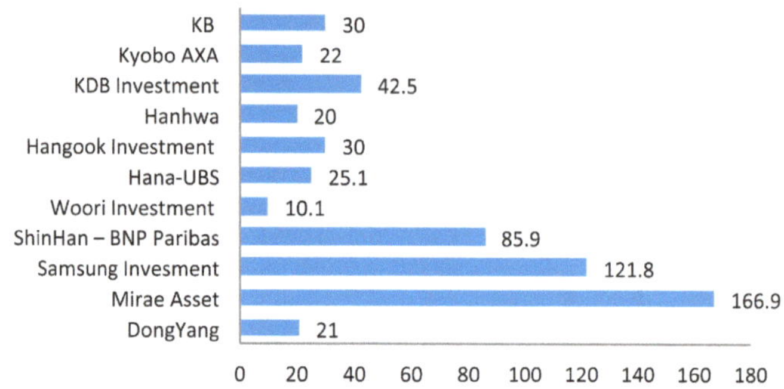

Figure 16: Total AUM by Company (in billions KRW)

Source: Chosun Biz

Figure 17: Strategy Composition by AUM

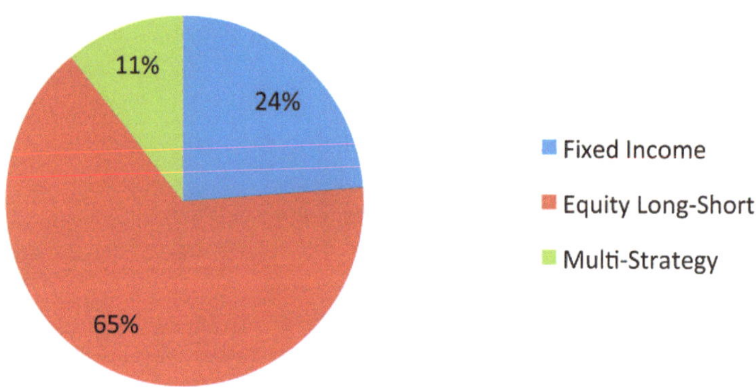

Source: Chosun Biz

GLOSSARY

Absolute return– The return that an asset achieves over a certain period of time. An absolute returns approach seeks to make positive returns regardless of market fluctuations. Contrasts with **relative return.**

Accredited investor– Class of investors who can engage in higher risk investments. Typically includes HNWIs and institutional investors. The specifications to be an accredited investor differs by each countries' laws.

Alpha– One of the five ratios to evaluate portfolio performance. Alpha is the value that the portfolio manager adds or subtracts to a fund's return. For example, a positive alpha of 5.0 indicates that the fund has outperformed the benchmark index by 5%. Likewise, the opposite is true with a negative alpha of 5.0.

Arbitrage– The act of profiting from price differences of an asset in different markets or forms. Arbitrage exists because of inefficiencies in the market.

Asset Management– The management of a client's investments by a financial services company.

Assets Under Management (AUM)– The market value of assets that an investment company manages on behalf of investors. It is used to measure success against the competition and consists of growth/decline due to both capital appreciation/losses and new money inflow/outflow.

Beta– The measure of the volatility or systematic risk of a portfolio compared to the market as a whole. It evaluates the security's tendency to be affected by market fluctuations. A beta higher than 1 indicates that the security will be less volatile than that of the market while a beta greater than 1 indicates greater volatility than that of the market.

Derivative– A form of security that is a contract between two or more parties. The value of the contract is derived from another asset called the underlying asset that can be stocks, futures, commodities, currency, or indices.

Family offices– Private wealth management company that only manages the assets and investments of a single family.

Fund of Hedge Funds– A diversified portfolio of hedge fund investments in which the fund manager chooses and invests in a number of hedge funds. This blending of different strategies and asset classes aims to provide a more stable long-term investment return than any of the individual funds.

Hedge Funds– A type of investment fund that can engage in wider range of investment and trading activities than other types of funds, but client base is generally limited to HNWIs and institutions.

Leverage– The use of different investment techniques to multiply gains and losses. These techniques can include borrowed capital or financial instruments. Leverage comes with risk as it magnifies the potential losses and gains.

Long Position– Buying a security (stock, commodity, currency) with the expectation that the asset will rise in value.

Long/short equity– A hedge fund strategy that utilizes both long and short positions in order to gain returns.

Mutual Funds– Professionally managed investment vehicle that collects capital from many investors in order to invest in securities. Mutual funds give small investors access to professionally managed and diversified portfolios.

Net Asset Value– Total value of the fund's portfolio (its assets), less its accrued liabilities (money owed to lending banks, fees owed to investment managers and service providers, and other liabilities).

Options– A type of derivative instrument that allows the buyer to buy an underlying security at a given price in the future. Underlying assets are typically stocks, bonds, currencies, or futures contracts.

Sharpe Ratio– It is a measurement commonly used to indicate risk-adjusted returns, calculated by subtracting the returns by the defined risk-free rate and dividing the result by the volatility—thus, a higher ratio correlates to a higher risk-adjusted return. It represents the amount return gained for each unit of risk the manager took. Some may consider it an unfair measure of a fund's performance because the ratio is calculated from the standard deviation of total return. It can be an appropriate tool to determine whether to add a fund to an existing portfolio. A better ratio to measure an individual portfolio's performance is the Sortino ratio.

Relative value– A method of assessing the value of an asset by taking into account the intrinsic value of the asset and comparing it to that of other assets.

Relative return– The returns of an asset are compared to a benchmark. More relevant for mutual funds.

Short position– Selling a borrowed security (stock, commodity, currency) with the expectation that the asset will fall in value.

Value Investment– The essence of value investing is buying stocks at less than their intrinsic value. For example, buying low PE ratio stocks, low price-to-cash-flow ratio stocks, or low price-to-book ratio stocks.

Volatility– A tool to measure the risk of a security. It measures the security's likelihood to go up or down in value. Higher volatility indicates greater propensity for swings in the value of the security and lower volatility indicates smaller propensity.

High Water Mark– The greatest point in the value of the portfolio. Hedge funds apply a high water mark to ensure that manager receive bonuses only after they reach the high watermark. It prevents compensation despite poor performance of the portfolio.

REFERENCES

i. "Harvard Endowment Rises $4.4 Billion to $32 Billion." 2011. *Harvard Magazine,* September 22. Accessed July 9, 2012. http://harvardmagazine.com/2011/09/harvard-endowment-rises-to-32-billion?page=all.

ii. "HFR Global Hedge Fund Industry Reports." 2012. *HFR Global Hedge Fund Industry Reports.* Hedge Fund Research. Accessed June 8, 2012.

iii. "Financial Market Series: Hedge Funds." *The City UK*, March 2012, 1–12.

iv. "Financial Market Series: Hedge Funds." *The City UK*, March 2012, 1–12.

v. Barclays Capital. 2011. *The Money Trail*: *Capital Solutions, Hedge Fund Intelligence.* Accessed July 10, 2012. http://barcap.info/static/BarCap/Attached Document/Hedge Fund Quarterly December 2011.pdf.

vi. Creswell, Julie. 2012. "Pensions Find Riskier Funds Fail to Pay Off." *New York Times*, April 2. Accessed June 3, 2012. http://www.nytimes.com/2012/04/02/business/pension-funds-making-alternative-bets-struggle-to-keep-up.html?_r=1.

vii. Teacher Retirement Service of Texas. 2012. *Performance Review: First Quarter 2012*.

viii. "Asia-Pacific Wealth Report 2011." 2011. *Capgemini & Merrill Lynch Wealth Management* 6: 1–36.

ix. "Rule 13h-1: Large Trader Reporting ." *Securities and Exchange Commission* , July 27, 2011. http://www.sec.gov/rules/final/2011/34-64976.pdf (accessed August 21, 2012).

x. "NET WORTH STANDARD FOR ACCREDITED INVESTORS ."*Securities and Exchange Commission* , December 21, 2011. http://www.sec.gov/rules/final/2011/33-9287.pdf (accessed August 21, 2012).

xi. "Overview and Evolution of the Institutional Market for Hedge Funds in Europe." 2012. *Preqin*: 1–20.

xii. "The Eurekahedge Report." *Eurekahedge*, March 2012. 1-32. Print.

xiii. "The Eurekahedge Report." *Eurekahedge*. March 2012: 1-32. Print.

xiv. "Here Are The Emerging Markets to Watch For In Asia."*Business Insider*. 9 May 2011: n. page. Web. 18 Jul. 2012. <http://articles.businessinsider.com/2011-05-09/wall_street/30100767_1_fund-managers-

xv. "China ups Asia hedge fund share to 30%." *Hedge Fund Journal*. 11 May 2012: n. page. Web. 18 Jul. 2012.

xvi. "No Time For Pity As Yong Rises To Top Of Asia Hedge Funds." *Bloomberg* . 28 March 2012: n. page. Web. 18 Jul. 2012. <http://www.bloomberg.com/news/2012-03-27/no-time-for-pity-as-yong-rises-to-top-of-asia-hedge-funds.html>.

xvii. "South Korea To Ease Hedge Fund Restrictions." August 1, 2012. Accessed August 21, 2012. http://www.finalternatives.com/node/21183

AIMA. 2012. http://www.aima.org/en/knowledge_centre/education/aima-journal/past-articles/index.cfm/jid/15C00C5D-B27A-4859-B5B1242E17vCB41A4.

Cameron, Bruce. "Hedge funds: proceed with care."*Personal Finance*, June 3, 2012. Accessed June 19, 2012. http://www.iol.co.za/business/personal-finance/columnists/bruce-cameron/hedge-funds-proceed-with-care-1.1310169Cayman Hedge Fund World, "Cayman Investment Fund Regulation." Last

modified 2009. Accessed August 20, 2012. http://www.
caymanhedgefundworld.com/html/categories.html.

"Chosun Biz." 2012. *Chosun Newspaper,* May 10. Accessed May 10, 2012.

"The Current Asian Hedge Fund Industry." 2012. *Investments &
Pensions Asia*, May 31. Accessed July 18, 2012. http://www.
ipe.com/asia/the-current-asian-hedge-fund-industry_45775.
php?articlepage=1.

de Sa'Pinto, Martin, and Tommy Wilkes. 2012. "Funds of hedge funds fight
to stay relevant." *Reuters*, May 28. Accessed May 28, 2012. http://
uk.reuters.com/article/2012/05/28/uk-financial-hedgefunds-
idUKLNE84R00T20120528.

Dodd-Frank Summary and News, "Dodd-Frank Summary." Last modified
2012.

Accessed May 23, 2012. http://doddfranksummary.com/the-dodd-
frank-act-summary.

GuideMeSingapore.com. 2012. "Singapore Seeks to Enhance Hedge Fund
Regulations." Accessed May 23. http://www.guidemesingapore.
com/blog-post/singapore-business/singapore-seeks-to-
enhance-hedge-fund-regulations.

Hyung-Gyu Shin. 2009. *Korea's Hedge Fund Story*. Seoul: Hans Media.

Ismail, Netty. "Singapore's New Hedge-Fund Regulation Puts City `Back On

Map." *Bloomberg*, July 29, 2010. Accessed May 23, 2012 http://www.
bloomberg.com/news/2010-07-28/singapore-hedge-fund-
regulations-lure-managers-put-city-back-on-the-map-.html.

Jaegar, Robert A. *All About Hedge Funds : The Easy Way to Get Started*.
United States of America: McGraw-Hill, 2003.

Khosla, Tanuj. "Here Are The Emerging Markets to Watch For In Asia."
Business Insider, May 9, 2011. Accessed July 18, 2012. http://articles.
businessinsider.com/2011-05-09/wall_street/30100767_1_
fund-managers-fund-assets-fund-investors.

KPMG, "Hong Kong - Regulation ." Last modified 2012. Accessed August
20, 2012. http://www.kpmg.com/global/en/issuesandinsights/

articlespublications/international-hedge-funds-survey/pages/ hong-kong-regulation.aspx.

Mallon, Bart.2010. "New BVI Hedge Fund Regulations Start 01/01/2011," *Hedge Fund Law Blog*, December 14. Accessed May 23, 2012. http://www.hedgefundlawblog.com/new-bvi-hedge-fund- regulations-start-01012011.html.

Millennium Wave Investments, "Hedge Fund Risks." Last modified 2012. Accessed August 20, 2012. http://www.mauldincircle.com/ investment-risks.

"Preqin Special Report:Institutional Investor Outlook for Hedge Funds in 2012." *Preqin*,

November 2011. Accessed May 23, 2012. http://www.preqin.com/docs/ reports/preqin_special_report_hedge_funds_2012.pdf

Rodgers, Donna. "The Dodd-Frank Act Requires Hedge Fund Investments in Compliance and Technology." *About.com Financial Services*. Accessed May, 23 2012. http://financialservices.about.com/ od/EthicsCompliance/a/The-Dodd-Frank-Act-Requires-Hedge- Fund-Investments-In-Compliance-And-Technology.htm.

"Singapore Tightens Hedge Fund Regulations. *Hedgeweek*, April 28 2010. Accessed May 22, 2012. http://www.hedgeweek. com/2010/04/28/44594/singapore-tightens-hedge-fund- regulations.

Wee, Gillian. 2012. "Texas Teachers Taking Alternative Investing to New Risks." *Bloomberg Businessweek*, June 6. Accessed July 9, 2012. http://www.businessweek.com/news/2012-06-06/texas- teachers-taking-alternative-investing-to-new-risks.

Yamazaki, Tomoko and Netty Ismail. 2012. "No Time For Pity As Yong Rises To Top Of Asia Hedge Funds." *Bloomberg*, March 28. Accessed July 18, 2012. http://www.bloomberg.com/news/2012-03-27/ no-time-for-pity-as-yong-rises-to-top-of-asia-hedge-funds. html.

ABOUT THE AUTHORS

Seunghyun Cho is a founding partner and fund manager at Leonie Hill Capital (LHC), a hedge fund headquartered in Singapore, with a presence in both South Korea and the United States. He specializes in the Asian and U.S. equities, futures, and options markets. He conducts extensive quantitative modeling on market-neutral trading strategies utilizing equity indices, risk management analysis, and portfolio management. In addition, he formulated NeuTrade, LHC's original market-neutral trading strategy.

Cho has a BSc in computer science and management from Handong Global University in South Korea. In addition, he has a graduate certificate in financial engineering from Stanford University and an executive certificate in Financial Institutions for Private Enterprise Development from the Harvard Kennedy School.

He can be reached at seunghyun.cho@leoniehillcapital.com.

Gina Heng is a partner at Leonie Hill Capital and leads the research department. She conducts both fundamental and technical analyses as well as researches on proprietary trading systems. She has experience in various research and analyst positions in the financial industry. Gina has a BA (political science and economics) from the University of Pennsylvania.

She can be reached at gina.heng@leoniehillcapital.com.

To find about Leonie Hill Capital, please visit www.leoniehillcapital.com.